Birds the Colours and Shapes of Leaves

by

Bob Toynton

HAMMERINN BOOKS

Published by Hammerinn Books

Achnacarry, Glenmore Road
Oban, Scotland   PA34 4PG

ISBN: 978-1-9999584-0-4

ACKNOWLEDGEMENTS

Some of these poems have appeared previously elsewhere.
"Jasmine on Mother's Day" (Gold Dust Magazine),
"Recognising Danger" and "Kyle" (Wurdplay).

Thanks to:
Adele C. Geraghty and Jamie Livingstone for poetic support, and to all those who have listened (willingly or not) to me read over the years. Also thanks to all those who have organised and attended the "Let's Make a Scene" events in Oban (at which many of these peoms have been performed), and to all the other writer friends I have made in this part of the world for giving me the confidence and the push to finally present my poetry in print. Finally thanks to David Moore for his support, proof reading and patience.

Dedication

To David for believing.

Contents

Whispers

Birds the colours and shapes of leaves
Sit amongst the summer foliage
But never sing.
See the branches gently move
With no breath of wind.

On rolling lowland hills, green sheep are scattered
By the darting, barking dogs
Of perplexed owners.
See the long grass move, the rushes part
The metal gates suddenly ring out.

In every stream, transparent fish
Drag sticks through the water,
Abetting the conspiracy of weeds and ducks.
See the eddies drift, the gravel stir
The circles on the surface without the rain.

In every crowd, in every queue
Men and women overhear tales
Of "them", of the "others".
See the people mill about, hear them whisper
"We are scared. That's how we know they are here!"

Travelling in Greece

A glance, a cool dark living room
Familiar yet strange,
Pictures clues to mysteries
The chairs rearranged.
Those sticky stamps of coffee cups
Encoded on the cloth.
The bare light bulb calls out at night
In Morse to every moth.

In shade old men from childhood held
Within this life-shared street,
All histories long bartered
Stored in words now obsolete.
Backgammon boards in cafe doors
Click 'cross cicadas beat.
A move taps out a memory
Each secret nears complete.

The sea casts runes in sun-baked sand
Then washes them with spray
Beneath a woman's naked feet,
Her man a touch away.
Their glances are a secret code
Akin to one I've met
But within a language I can't know,
In an alien alphabet.

I sit exhausted by a road
Not marked on any chart.
Each signpost takes an age to read.
Some know the map by heart.
The path I've walked has broken up
Lost in the map's torn crease.
I feel I've spent so much of life
Just travelling in Greece.

Recognising Danger

Where is the danger?
Ignore it. I try.
It rustles behind me.
I miss it sneak by.

Shadows surround me.
I stumble and fall.
"An accident officer.
I saw no-one at all.

It must have been my fault,
It happened so quick.
Just walking. Not looking,
I tripped on a stick.

I slid down this gravel,
Where lodged on tough roots
With soles facing upwards,
A pair of old boots.

Doc Martens? The patterns
In purple on skin?
Well, this shirt's just a cheap one.
My jersey's so thin.

The blood? Oh, I see now,
It must be a graze.
My clumsiness officer?
It's only a phase."

A Whitewashed Cottage

A whitewashed cottage
Flies and the smell of seaweed
The East Neuk at its sun-baked best
On a late June morning a baby is born
Too early, weeks too early
Still and silent.

Poor mother was scared by cows the women said
Slap then silence
Born with a caul hiding a blue face
He'll never drown, the local fishermen said
Slap then silence.

Born this way he can never die at sea
But first he has to live.
They are all gone now, the fishermen.
A final slap and I started to cry
I would not stop
I might never stop.

Nystagmus

Looking up
Cries harden to screams.

Black ceiling patch
You who will grow with me
To become a map of Africa
It isn't you.

Once-rich curtains
Colours smoked
It isn't you.

Air sharp with the tang
Of scorched cotton
It isn't you.

Clumsy safety-pin
In blunt fingers
It isn't you.

Raised voices
Drowning my squalls
It isn't you.

Faces looking into mine
It can't be you.

(Did you ever look?
Did you never see?)

Too young for words
Too small for gestures
Helpless like a turtle
Facing up towards the bulb

Eyes unfocussed
Wide, vibrating,
Staring into swimming, reeling
Scalding light.

Linoleum Rarely Fills my Waking Thoughts

Linoleum rarely fills my waking thoughts.
I never stop to think about the patterns seen
But just a tattered square in a cold attic brought
The smell of doctors' waiting rooms and distant
Wintergreen -
The cloying dampness of Scottish winter coats –
To mind.
The burnt dust dry electric fire
One bar on, two off.
The still-innocent veils of Woodbine smoke afloat
In pale blue bands
Which buckled with each cough.
Eyes half-closed, the tin-car angled race track in the hall,
The sputnik and the dog's head no longer formed
Remaining undefined,
Having lodged themselves as memory of memory
Like Russian dolls,
As lino upon lino
Or paper under paper under paper,
Shaping woodchip walls.

The smell of beech leaves rarely floods my senses.
I never walk the countryside in hope to catch it on
the breeze
But the childhood garden hedge regrows
And later fences fade with just one breath

When I stumble upon autumn trees,
And the steep woods to the river reappear in frosty
mist
Through which the path-maze leads to Wallace's
castle
And the wishing well down which we'd throw round
stones
And peer for splashes far below
While in the close-by ferns a rustle
Would lead us to a pheasant or a deer
In undergrowth so damp our dens would drip
And camp fire flames when first alight just steamed
and hissed.
Our go-carts of nailed fish-boxes with the Arbroath
stamp
Would disintegrate on darkening root-crossed tracks,
But just in sight, the first street lamp.

I've looked down on the white-tipped summits of the
Pyrenees
And there again, the winters when it snowed and
snowed and snowed.
Piled shoulder high, the gently sloping geographies
of the big freeze,
The mountain ranges dividing pavement from the
road
Eroding between each daily flight to village school
despite the cold.
Through weeks each peak appointed its own name.
Each trickle formed a mighty stream,
Each icy patch, a hidden mountain pool.

A simple love of snow and landform captured in
frieze-frame;
A coldness far beyond the cool, encased within the
polished boots
Unthought of, but still unforgot,
Footprints on new lino floor; the ten year old.
With thaw the childish mountains left no trace,
Devoid of gnarled and ancient root,
But through the cleft between the now and not quite
yet they pour,
Tomorrow's memories. Unrecognised. Mute.

The Big Warm Dog

Beneath the steep rust-smelling bank
The grass is dusty and reddened.
Lank summer nettles loll
To the sound of white water.
There is no breeze
Only the rising and falling
Of midges in the shade.

The river is old and powerful
As it laps against the beach
Of oval bloodshot quartz
And flattened schist like salmon skins.

Out of the sun
The warm black dog daydreams
His ears hunting for familiar sounds
Amongst the words of the man
At the water's edge
Who stares at the float which never dips.

He never uses proper bait.
A worm maybe. Maybe not.
A fish if accidentally caught
Is swiftly killed
On the dark red stone glinting
With mica and scales.

As he stares at the water
Coughs tug hard
Like fishing-line hooked
Beneath the scars that time
Too slowly fades
And those he never talks about
Except here, to the river
And the big warm dog.

The Heron

Below old rocks the waters writhe
And heavy whirlpools slowly drift
As pebbles clash and stutter news
Of distant rain.

The heron guards the river's edge
Searching past the layers of light
His vision fractured, swirling now
His prey obscured.

And yet for dreams he, patient, waits
Still watcher of the lifeless flood
As sap-filled branches cartwheel by
So newly robbed

From crippled trees which point and sway
And part the air to make it whine
As the mountain stabs and roughly tears
The panicked clouds.

Moving

We had talked about it sensibly
Like the logistics of once more moving house.
You never feared death even before
You grew blind and impatient.
We knew there could be pain.
There was pain.

But confusion wasn't in the scheme.
Your body came unlocked like a family home
abandoned
And cleared carelessly by strangers
Room by room, all within one day.
The furniture in which you stored your shyness
Suddenly gone.

Those final words, over and over,
Loud, in a way that only the deaf can be.
Was it nervousness or an apology
For straying from some tidy plan,
Or taking up so many people's Thursday afternoon?
Again and again, the words "Oh dear".

Jasmine on Mother's Day

I.

I wanted to bring you a delicate wisp of the outside
world;
Sounds like liquid trickling metal beads
Half mercury, half amber,
Shaped from the air of my garden by the goldfinches
You could never see.

I wanted to bring you the light that had passed
unaltered
Through the perfect crystal
On my hallway shelf
Only to be startled into colour by a bubble of water
Trapped in its heart.

I wanted to bring you air,
A parcel of air
Scented with air
Diluted with air
And full of the beautiful
Impurities of the world.

Your vision had become heavy
With the shadow of stones.
Shingle crunched in your ears
And I brought you jasmine
With its scent: soapy, dense,
Polished and round
Like pebbles for your nose.

II.

Inadvertently I brought you a measure of your life.
The scented pebbles
Scarcely noticed out of doors
Scattered around your living room
Recording by their depth and distribution
The opening of windows
And then, only of doors.

You moved it after a week to the hallway
Where pebbles were trampled out as helpers
Came and went.
Others tumbled carelessly.
The stairs became even more
Perilous and heady.

When I returned to your house that day,
Before I found the unmade bed,
The sheets clumsily folded back
In your own darkness,
The washing-up you could never leave,
And the half-drunk nocturnal mug of tea
Abandoned,

I opened the door to a creeping, shifting
Bank of scree,
And sank until it held my legs
And pressed my lungs
And groping there
For air, for light, for company
Were the jasmine's tendrils
Pale, almost broken,
And me.

III.

We planted it in my garden,
All of your children.
It has been given the chance of a different life
And reaches now in all directions
Exploring for the perfect crystals
Far beneath our keenest sight
While tangling with the moving air
And the goldfinches in swooping flight.

I know that even this in time
Will falter and cease its climbing,
But I'll seek the flowers, white and waxen,
Self-effacing by the wall,
And that landslide of fragrance the small flower
imparts
Precariously hung in its fragile frame
Of leaves like a ladder of long stretching hearts.

Kyle

Like the heavy slapping
flapping splash of canvas
wet in a dawn breeze,
he rose from the edge of a hidden pool
amongst the rocks and gently swelling wrack
- and blew -
like the ghost of a fisherman
along the shore.

In the narrows, a wave
- dark - too smooth, too heavy,
rolled and slid amongst the foam,
as the silkie - swollen, night's work done,
tired of the air and a woman's skin
 - swam slowly
beyond the reach of the tethered land
to patient sea.

Swept by tides
to this place where the sea's clasped hands
- struggling - hold the hills apart,
I was met by the heron
- myself - my once lost friend,
and together we watched the silkie
and the souls depart.

Woken by the Evening Sun

As worn as distant memories
The ice-smoothed shoulder yields at last
To evening sun.
Though pale at noon the cotton-grass,
Now a thousand torches lit,
Parts to mark the muddy path
To where the lochan laps and sucks
Its fragile shore.

Only in these late June days
The dark screes of the northern face
Ripple in the slanting light
As first the mountain, cold and slow,
Leans, or does it reach to me,
Through air as clear as new-made glass.
Sharp shadows shifting sifting thoughts
Of strength and age beyond my grasp.

No youthful brilliance startles here,
Just richly ambered setting Sun,
While the summit lifts and gently glows
As only an evening mountain can.
Bashful against the reddening sky
Once solid ridges buckle as they're kissed,
While on their stretching shadows swing
Boulders heavy as the past.

And though I know that all is still
I sense slow movement granite-deep.
In ancient cratons crystals ache and tear
As the mountain, silent, with the softest breath
Rolls the cool now midge-filled air
And seems to pull the deep-wove peat
Close around its craggy chin
As it settles back to sleep again.

Crail Harbour

Cobbled Shoregate turns and tumbles
Like water searching for the open sea
Squeezing between the sandstone cottages
Before spilling onto the harbour quay

With its weed-hung slabs of ancient wall
Wedged tight against the rising tide
Like a hand near-closed against all dangers
Fishing boats huddle safe inside.

Unloaded creels and mismatched boxes
Contents crawling, sliding, slithering, still
Are watched by gulls from the pantiled rooftops
Their ghostly flapping, their cruel calls shrill

Cut through the air made dense by diesel
And the tang of seaweed, fish and crab:
The sights and sounds and smells of fishing
Before the boats grew large and drab.

And even though great storms break landward
And dark shadows up the gables climb
The stones stand strong through wave and wind
While all else is swept clean by thoughtless time.

Winter in North Norfolk

Cold sky and marsh and sea entangled
With wind unshaped through lack of sails
Full measured by the sky-still seagull
Head curved as a Viking prow.

Coarse gravel ridges breaking northwards
Clutching gorse and hedge and heath,
This poor windbreak for Suffolk's prairie,
Spilling flints fill cold grey sea.

Through salt-burned pines and last year's grasses
The sharp sand singing antique tongues
Calling Celt, Iceni, Roman, Dane from
Far across the pagan fields

Where churches hide in shallow hollows
Alive with rooks but blind with trees
Their stones grown cold through careless ages,
Villageless.

Alone.

Alone.

Living with Tolstoy

You were Levin, your love anxious
Timid as starlight
When you first called her Kitty.
She, the intricate ice on dark frozen soil,
You the shy winter Sun.

You were Pierre, your passions vast
And clumsy as Russia
When you first called her Natasha.
She, the innocent spring Moon playing in the trees,
You the beckoning bright glade.

Too fierce for one woman,
One family, one nation,
In summer your love shattered
Like sunlight striking a holy icon;

Colours dancing as aurora
Thrown around the world,
Whilst she sat here in candlelight
Measuring your heavy words.

Now you are Karenin, your love
As certain and cruel as the law.
No not Anna
She has always been Sonya.

Poor Sonya, her place is here.
Another awaits you at the station.
It is late autumn now
And she is begging you not to go.

No-Man's Land

Come and see me at rest.
At last I have found in this cold table
The hard edge of the past.
I bear a name too late for the village memorial,
Yet dying too soon I passed unnoticed.

You see before you
Part man, part history.
Too frail to leave a mark on stone.
Proof if proof you need that death is not the end,
For this is my second, my third, my fourth.

You called me
"Institutionalised". No!
I just let go
Lingering on in No-Man's Land hoping to find a
comrade
No longer grinning but whole and smiling.

I was not in a hospital
Through four decades of noisy silence,
For there is no cure for those departed.
I was here in my place of safety, my refuge, my
asylum
Grim and solid, built amidst the memory of muddy
fields.

The Doubts of Paul the Anchorite

As if the night itself congeals
Drops appear from thin still air
Silent swellings on the stone
Until each globe, each doubt, each care
Falls ungainly through the gloom
To fill anew the hidden pool
Ploot, ploot, ploot, ploot.
Careless of saint or holy fool.

Worshipped for their very age,
Old gods now sleep, now slip away
As statues stuck with wax and dust
Glower dark with grim decay
Yet even so in sun-seared streets
As wine from toppled jars still drips
Ploot, ploot, ploot, ploot.
Saturn sings through drunken lips.

Eris, brother, malformed twin
Was it you who forced my sudden flight
To this broken land, this lonely cave
Where Venus is but a distant light
Now pure, now cold upon my bed,
Or was I brought by a stronger will
Ploot, ploot, ploot, ploot.
To where water mocks a time grown still?

The night sky filled with antique myths
Washed clean each day by brilliant light
As waves of faith and sand sweep in
Which smooth my visions and my sight.
But as I starve the ancient ones
They drip their questions in my ear,
And now the one that I most fear,
Ploot, ploot, ploot, ploot.
O am I born or buried here?

Shaving with Thomas Huxley

A small disc of purest chalk
Fashioned by a machine we never see
Its existence witnessed only by this dot.
Placed carelessly on the tablemat
(Bought in a Sunday market -
Farmyard scenes of long ago)
It gives by fateful chance
A wall-eye to the cheerful golden calf.

Collected in slippered, not sandalled feet,
With eyes barely awake, flickering in pale cool light.
In place of awesome thunderous storm
The timid squeak of a cupboard door
And there it sits. The Tablet.

A word white on white
Carved, grinning just beyond my morning sight
It could be "hold"
It could be "fooled"
No space here for a Decalogue
No "Honour thy father and thy mother"
Fine. I can't do both.

Huxley and Wilberforce, modern and smooth, argue still,
While Darwin dwells on why he looks,
All silver hair and flowing beard, like God,
Not ape.

That's it!
The word is "old."
Reflecting glass confirms the truth.

"If the beard were all, the goat may preach."
Words of wisdom and foolishness and age
Impossible to untangle.
I shave my head.
I shave my chin.
I swallow my tiny chalky pill.

The Prodigal

Like an uncertain guest who sits close by the door
Dressed as for mourning in black and old gold
Dulled by the deaths of those who would share
Your age-obscured stories; the power you once held.

So dear an acquaintance of those I once loved,
Their favour and feelings no longer at risk,
I come to disturb you, at least with my thoughts,
These decades of questions I now dare to ask.

Come through, sit beside me. Let's talk of the past,
Before you grew ancient. Before you found love.
Of old you spoke often of bloodshed and fear,
Of plagues and disasters and those you helped save.

You said some were chosen, so the others were not.
But who did the choosing? Could favour be earned?
Your words full of desert, of salt and of dust,
Spoke of children struck down and of cities which
burned.

You said that the rabbit and pig are unclean.
And that we should not eat of their meat.
Nor the blood of any creature on Earth,
There goes my bacon and black pudding treat.

Not funny, your words. Oh, of that I'm aware
That humour makes human you could never
conceive
It was snake, man and woman that gave birth to sin
but now you blame Adam and Steve.

While those who kept slaves did not sin in your eyes
Abomination, abhorrent were the words you called
me
You said that my kind should die for their love
What could I do but take that personally.

 "Those times are so distant. Those thoughts now so
old
The world has moved forward. The language
evolved.
You cannot now blame me for what I once said.
Time changes all things including my words."

But you have not disowned them. Cast them aside.
They give succour to those who would injure and kill
For words can be sharpened and wielded like knives
By those who still love you. Or so they would claim.

"But if they still loved me then surely they'd know
I have tried to convince them for all that I'm worth
To discount the words they once put in my mouth.
I've done all that I could do. I've moved Heaven and
Earth.

I can't wipe out hatred. I can't make them love.
I can only tell stories and hope they believe.
Old pages were challenged. A new leaf was turned.
A testament written for a new way to live.

I know you are nervous of my presence here,
But don't blame a book for the harm people do.
I've been part of your family for so many years.
Just a nice warm dry corner. I'll be quiet. I'll be
good."

We have a shared history, so I suppose you should
stay
Though so much of your past just fills me with
shame
As an unwitting weapon for the bigots to wield
It is you who are the prodigal; but this is your home.

Poles Apart

Poles
Apart, they argue on with facts
As cold as snow and hard as ice, ignored until
More temperate natures cut the carbon curse some
Thought insane, in Paris, where the pavement cafes, avenues
And bridges glisten still with acid rain. Some see the Earth, a fragile
Ark adrift in deepest empty space, while others see this robust globe
Of God's design, where scientists and thinkers all should know their place.
While ancient ice-caps melt and glaciers crack and crash into warming seas
As symptoms of the planet's dangerous fever. Listen! You can hear it sneeze
Hurricanes grow ever stronger, while droughts and wild-fires scorch the land
The cards are stacked against the planet, and we now hold the weaker hand.
The sceptics point to the poorest people with promised jobs in coal and oil
The atmosphere should cure itself they say, without a risk to fragile soil.
"Ecosystems, environment" they're just nonsense spoken by the asinine
Who think profit can mean something other than the bottom line.
Those politicians who refuse to see the shape this planet's in
Why would we ever vote for you; believe your spin?
Play our cards right, you, not the Earth gets
Dumped. Bugger! A neat trick.
Trumped.

Losing Lyonesse

You say that though I cannot see
I must now hear the shingle roar just steps away.
I hear the roar, I hear the cracks
From deep within the dark-leaf woods
As creatures move through Lyonesse,
As creatures die in Lyonesse.

Within this dark the dreams bring forth
Old journeys to the left of dawn
Where all the day the sun kept low
And barely warmed the broken rock
Across that painless frost-cut land,
That numb, that painless frost-cut land.

Throughout the times of colder air
When trees and grass were all newborn
The land reached for the setting sun
As sapling birch like feathers blew
And rippled in the moss-edged pools,
The clear reflecting moss-edged pools.

I heard my mother's mother tell
Of pack-ice growling on the shore
Which caught and held the awesome power
Of every wave the winter flung
Against the plain of Lyonesse,
Sweet-water plain of Lyonesse.

But those grim banks of shingled flint
Each spring crept by where willows grew
And salt slow poisoned pool by pool
And earth grew hungry for the tread
Of mammoth, wolf and deer,
For mammoth wandered here.

You ask me now what we must do
As salt-dulled pebbles rattle close
And soon may block the wattled door.
Go choose the posts too good to leave
And tie them with harsh heather rope,
Harsh moorland woven heather rope.

And load them high with weighty cloth
And all that's good for upland life
For the roaring sea won't follow you
Amongst the polished granite hills
Where mud-pools swallow those who stray,
And mud-pools keep all those who stray.

But I will stay for my lost sight
Lives on in forests long decayed
In clearings lit with asphodel
Around the lily-frosted pools
Before the shingle killed the land,
It bruised my eyes and killed the land.

And it may be this storm which takes
Me back across the drowning plain,
And dreaming, drift through salty glades
Where in the blackness I may sense
Why we are losing Lyonesse,
For we are losing Lyonesse.

Flags of Difference

Mohammed lost his Facebook friends today
One by one the numbers trickled down
Why they unfriended, well who could say
No-one would even answer the phone.

Of course he'd been spat on in the street
This is a Christian country after all
But at work he'd been feted as one of the elite
With an office, a degree and an important role.

Well read on Kant and Marx and Proust
Intellectual, modest and quietly spoken
By all the right causes he'd been seduced
With a sincerity no-one could ever question.

He was Paris. His face red, white and blue
Even "I am Charlie" he had cautiously said,
Then "Je suis Bruxelles. Je saigne pour vous."
Like all his friends he turned black, yellow and red.

But now his friends appear to be no more
A tactless step. Doesn't he know his place?
Presumptuously he typed the words "I am Lahore"
With a green flag and crescent on his face.

Pink Granite

Let's not talk of millions,
Of whole nations.
Let's not talk of tens of thousands
Or even of hundreds.
For this was an individual horror,
Each one alone.

Here is granite
Hard and cold,
Grey at first glance,
Seen only by those who look down,
By those who already know;
For this is a secret monument.

Two large triangles pass as pavement.
The other, posing as steps to the canal
Stands out.
One shameless slab has been damaged
By the hammer blow
That no-one heard.

Here the eye is not led to the heavens
But down to dark water,
Tainted and poorly reflecting.
There is no sanctuary,
No space kept clear for thought,
For this is a cenotaph of trampled souls.

Kneel down. Touch. There is no dirt,
No whispered contagion here,
Even though the granite is not grey
But flushed timid pink,
Faded through age and neglect
From the badges of the Third Reich.

No words here of death
Only of oppression.
No words here of the camps
Only of persecution.
No words here of the gas chambers
Only of suffering.

Who would the truth offend?
Surely not those who walk through,
Or over this place of the redacted dead,
Or pass by on the other side,
Their consciences prepared and raw
For the justly guilt-filled house nearby

Where, from other hidden spaces,
A young girl and her family
Were dragged back into a world
Where death was yellow,
Purple, red, black, green
And gentle blushing embarrassed pink.

A Long Way from Ararat

The fearsome crackle of lightning overhead
Had subsided to a distant growl
In dank uneasy sky of lead
      When glancing up
          I saw above
              Afloat on wings about to fail

    A pure white dove.

Crash-landing in an olive tree close by
It shook its wings of melting snow.
Lifting up my paper I looked at the crossword.
      Off it flew!
          'It must be tired'
             I thought, and now

    A cryptic clue.

Cerberus and Me

Where once dust rich with heavy spices hung,
Disturbed by sandalled foot of Byzantine or Jew,
Now tramp the weary Euro-hordes amongst
Which sweat and stumble I, but never you.

Proud outer walls betray a tumbled town
Of barrel vaults collapsed, long open to the sun.
Where vines sag dark with shrivelled grapes turned
brown
The 'merchant' now sells postcards - 'Greece is Fun!'

Upon a step, in shade you, snoring, slept
With muzzle turned both white and sandy as the
stone.
No guard upon the entrance was there kept,
For many raised their feet yet I alone

Sat down to eat black olives, drink cold beer
And tried to rouse you from your dreamful twitching
sleep.
Slow-opened eye, stiff stretch just made it clear
That door-guards crumble with the doors they keep.

I drift to heroes of the mythic past
When all that we imagine could be true.
Come Bellerophon! Fleet Pegasus! At last
Awake! - Just the old card-seller, me and you.

In living we all mould to shapes around us,
As you now fit your time-worn step with ease,
But if you dare claim descent from mighty Cerberus
Then you may call me Perseus or even Hercules.

Performativity

The Ark of the Cacophony
Slaps through a heat-pressed sea
The sun erodes the islands
Whole islands cease to be.

Bouzouki banshees bray aboard
Above the diesel drone
While passengers talk two by two
By two. I sit alone.

Clutching on a German word - a phrase
Some French comes wheeling by,
While children fight in ageless Greek
I stick to stateless 'Hi!'

As they raise up a paper each
The J's give Dutch away.
I catch a glance in English
But then Italian takes the day.

Becalmed upon a Babel-boat
I launch a strategy.
Today I'll be Icelandic;
Tomorrow I'll pretend to be me.

Agamemnon's Tomb

The children of your thoughts but not your blood,
Unknowing of Thyestes, pass you by
For the Lion Gate which offers only shade,
Avoiding ancient curses where you lie.

A startled bird rings out a piercing call
As if to warn that I have lost my way.
Did dogs or geese or faithless Capricorn
Cry out to you of victory's decay?

Travelling

As the priest carelessly shuffled his feet
The lily leaves shredded into tattered islands
On the dusty floor.

The woman, unknowing, crossed herself
As the bus lurched past each wayside shrine,
And the radio stammered football scores
In age-worn Greek.

The window cast her haloed face
Into the earth-stuffed ancient olive groves.
The hillsides seemed to know her well
As they swayed across her story-face
And kissed her cheek goodbye.

The Collector

Why am I so grateful
That you know my name
From years ago?
There's nothing left at all
To interest you in this plain
Un-haunted room
Scattered with dust-bleached mementoes
Placed just so like trophies
In a dark wood hall of unknown shape
Un-shadowed in the gloom.

There's no response
From old wood caressed
It's life-proof grain long lost
Beneath stale polish
But here and there some metal glints
In answer to your thoughtless touch
And as before the breakages
The costs
Are mine to bear
But you must own the fingerprints.

Damn your brain! Yield just one nerve
To tell me why you come
Confess. It's not for my collection you return
It's for the past.
I realise now you never knew
I stole from you a joy in life
And wrote verse to hide my happiness.
I thought I'd escaped detection
And so I saved the lines.
Do you remember how they go?

Jupiter

"The strange noise from the radio is Jupiter" I was
told as a child.
"He was a god".
I listened.
It made no sense.

I don't know how - or what - to call you.
Every name I know has been touched.

It's February.
Jupiter freezes in the sky.
Spinning shards of hard-edged light
Clink and stab the window-glass
Priming scores of short-wave holes
With jutting wires of ice.

Filament and crystal sing
Like sharp-tuned nerves.

Another day I didn't phone, didn't fight.
Valentine's night.

Too many imaginary friends
Make my call unwelcome
As they circle you.

Later they comfort me
Rewinding slowly, coldly
These bandages of stormy light.

Half a Fishing Net

"Half a fishing net"
The statement catches me by surprise
For though the road outside runs deep
And my thoughts are dredging through the past
To trust these words must be unwise.

Once headphones clamped to teenage ears
With volume turned up all the way
Drowning out the slamming doors
The weekend fights, the screams, the tears
My head, the cave in which I aim to stay.

Scalpel-bright the hard, clear voice
Asks Alice when she's ten feet tall
Paring imperceptibly
The bandwidth of the aural nerves
White rabbits run before a fall.

Big Brother rumbles, roars and thrills
As Janis pleads, emotions multiply
Beyond the desperate frantic screams
Until she teases tears from the very stones
And I curl up tight and start to cry.

"Half a fishing net"
Have we talked of late of harbour days?
It seems to make such little sense
Though we went to visit Crail last month
I remember, and then my mind replays

December on the Anfield Kop
My comfort zone nowhere in sight.
Men, more men, and even more
Pressed like stones, compressed and arched
Too closely packed to even fight.

Singing shouting cursing hard
Members of an alien tribe.
Ears deafened, numbed (I own no scarf).
Feet no longer touching solid ground
I turn within; turn off and hide.

"Half a fishing net"
I'm sure that's what he said
Are we having trout or salmon for our tea
With nylon tangled in silvered scales?
But it's me that's nearly lost my thread.

It's January in a Liverpool concert hall
Deep rhythmic thudding shakes the crowd
Now melded, melted by roaring noise
The walls and floor and air vibrate
No remission is requested or allowed.

Guitar attacked with a violin bow
And the pathos of the electric blues
Shrieks and streaks to the stratosphere,
As voice and strings compete to split
The heart, the ear, perhaps the atom too.

I brave King Crimson, Groundhogs, Stone the Crows
But Led Zeppelin with such thunderous force
Shake each person loose to their inner world
While in the States, Charles Richter sighs
I tumble inward and sing 'til hoarse.

"Half a fishing net"
My mind now reels and casts about in vain
It's clear I just don't catch the drift
If I'm going to wriggle off this hook
I'll wait to hear it called again.

My mother's hearing ebbed away
And long ago I was duly warned
For in her later years it mostly disappeared
Old age was all that she could blame
But I take comfort in my deafness being earned.

No gentle fog, no cotton wool
Marks growing distance from every sound
For I clearly hear the slightest noise
But with gaps unrecognised the brain steps in
And fills them carelessly with words new-found.

"Half a fishing net". Ah, I understand
For I recognise now my own predictive text.
"Yes, I'm on the final verse at last", I reply.
"Have I finished yet?
Nearly. But why so vexed?"

Loving the Man with P. T. S. D.

I want to walk into your nightmare.
To join you in the geography I have learned
By joining the dots
Of your murmurs and cries.
There in the vortex I will stand,
Fears like sharp grit blasting against me,
The metal blades of your memories
Whirling and scything the air.
But they are your fears, your memories.
They strike but cannot harm me.
Like a small human planet
I will let the debris of your past accrete.
Passively I will gather it in
And let it fuse layer upon layer
A new outer shell of rock and steel
Hard against the world outside.
Don't be scared by the silence now,
The unexpected emptiness.
Beneath this carapace it is cosy
Come and join me in my sleep.
Let us call the warmth, love.
Let us call this new space home.
Let us bring the cat tomorrow night
And settle in.

The Promise

It's something that can't be caught
It just happens.
It's something that can't be described
It just is.
It is something that can't be measured
Save by the scale and intensity
Of the void it leaves behind.

Promise me
That you will never cause me to know
The sheer breadth and depth of my love for you.
I promise you the same.

Rebel without a clue

Today I decided to rebel
I wore odd socks
But both were black

So what the hell
I shaved my head
The hair grew back.

How would I look
With a tattoo on my arm.
Something brash and gory?

Don't be alarmed
Knowing me
It would just say 'S O R R Y'.

www.ingramcontent.com/pod-product-compliance
Lightning Source LLC
Chambersburg PA
CBHW061805050726
47598CB00002B/891